Meals Around the World

Meals in Germany

by R.J. Bailey

Bullfrog Books

Ideas for Parents and Teachers

Bullfrog Books let children practice reading informational text at the earliest reading levels. Repetition, familiar words, and photo labels support early readers.

Before Reading
- Discuss the cover photo. What does it tell them?
- Look at the picture glossary together. Read and discuss the words.

Read the Book
- "Walk" through the book and look at the photos. Let the child ask questions. Point out the photo labels.
- Read the book to the child, or have him or her read independently.

After Reading
- Prompt the child to think more. Ask: Have you ever eaten German food? Were the flavors new to you? What did you like best?

Bullfrog Books are published by Jump!
5357 Penn Avenue South
Minneapolis, MN 55419
www.jumplibrary.com

Copyright © 2017 Jump! International copyright reserved in all countries. No part of this book may be reproduced in any form without written permission from the publisher.

Library of Congress Cataloging-in-Publication Data

Names: Bailey, R.J., author.
Title: Meals in Germany / by R.J. Bailey.
Description: Minneapolis, Minnesota: Jump!, Inc. [2016] | © 2017 | Series: Meals around the world "Bullfrog Books are published by Jump!."
Audience: Ages 5–8. | Audience: K to grade 3.
Includes bibliographical references and index.
Identifiers: LCCN 2016014180 (print)
LCCN 2016014582 (ebook)
ISBN 9781620313725 (hardcover: alk. paper)
ISBN 9781620314906 (pbk.)
ISBN 9781624964190 (ebook)
Subjects: LCSH: Food—Germany—Juvenile literature. | Cooking, German—Juvenile literature. Food habits—Germany—Juvenile literature.
Classification: LCC TX721 .B2344 2016 (print)
LCC TX721 (ebook) | DDC 394.1/20943–dc23
LC record available at http://lccn.loc.gov/2016014180

Editor: Jenny Fretland VanVoorst
Series Designer: Ellen Huber
Book Designer: Leah Sanders
Photo Researchers: Kirsten Chang, Leah Sanders

Photo Credits: All photos by Shutterstock except: Getty, 8–9, 14, 16–17.

Printed in the United States of America at Corporate Graphics in North Mankato, Minnesota.

Table of Contents

Oma's Spaetzle	4
Make Spaetzle!	22
Picture Glossary	23
Index	24
To Learn More	24

Oma's Spaetzle

Wake up, Ann!

It's morning in Germany.

It's time for breakfast.

Ann has muesli.

She puts milk on it.

7

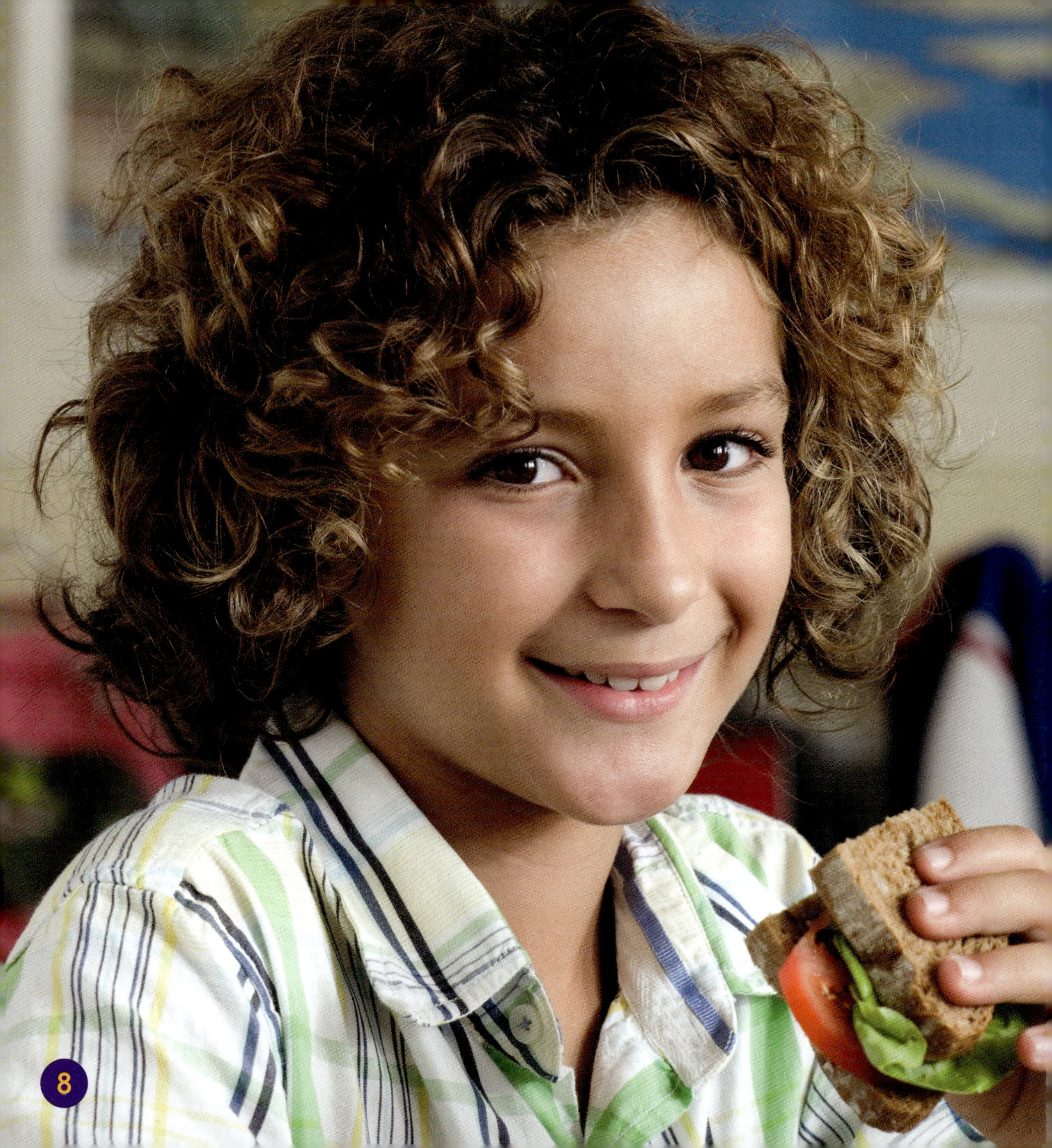

Lars is at school.

It is time for a snack.

He eats a sandwich.

Erik is home for lunch.
Oma makes spaetzle.

Yum! It is good.

She makes schnitzel, too.
Erik eats it with potatoes.
Lunch is a big meal!

13

It is a special day.

Hans wants a treat.

He buys a bratwurst.

16

He buys a pretzel.
Wow! It is big.

It is dark. We have a light dinner.

We eat bread, meat, and cheese.

19

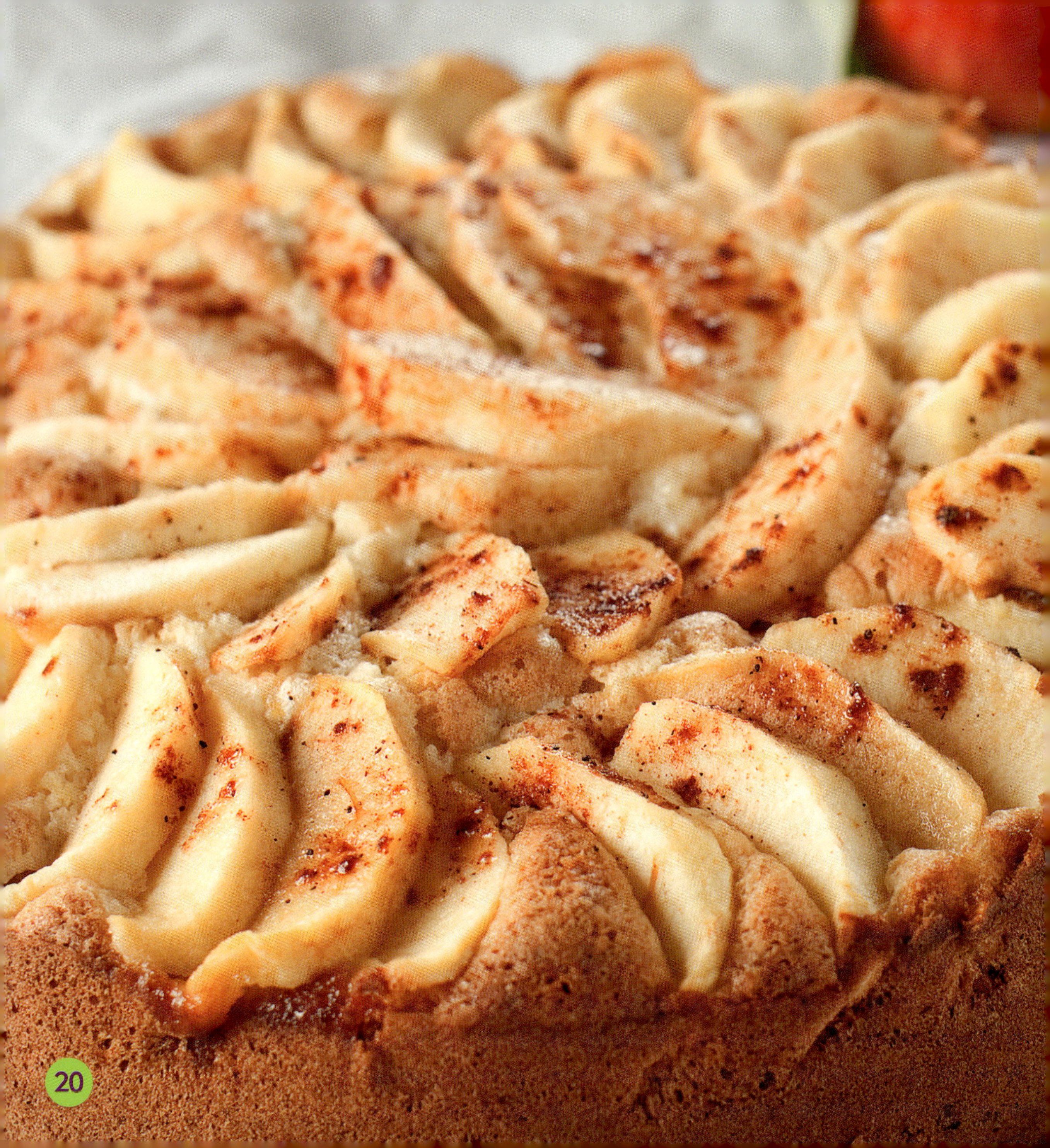

We have kuchen.
Max likes Black Forest.
Pia likes apple. Yum!

Make Spaetzle!

Make German dumplings! Be sure to get an adult to help.

Ingredients:
- 2¼ cups flour
- 1 tsp salt
- 2 large eggs
- ½ to 1 cup water

Directions:
1. Mix flour and salt in a bowl.
2. Add eggs. Mix well.
3. Slowly add water to make a smooth and firm dough.
4. Let the dough stand for 10 minutes. Bring a big pot of salted water to a boil.
5. Push the dough through the biggest holes of a cheese grater into the boiling water.
6. The dumplings will float when they are done. Remove them with a slotted spoon.
7. Serve with diced bacon or fried onions. You can also toss them with shredded cheese.
8. Enjoy!

Picture Glossary

bratwurst
A German sausage that is fried or grilled.

Oma
The German word for grandmother.

kuchen
The German word for cake.

pretzel
A hard bread that is salted and usually shaped like a loose knot.

muesli
A mixture of oats, fruits, and nuts.

schnitzel
A thin slice of meat that is covered with breadcrumbs and fried.

Index

Black Forest 21
bratwurst 15
breakfast 6
dinner 18
kuchen 21
lunch 10, 12
muesli 6
pretzel 17
sandwich 9
schnitzel 12
snack 9
spaetzle 10

To Learn More

Learning more is as easy as 1, 2, 3.

1) Go to www.factsurfer.com

2) Enter "mealsinGermany" into the search box.

3) Click the "Surf" button to see a list of websites.

With factsurfer.com, finding more information is just a click away.